Silver Jubilee

"where must we go, we who wander this wasteland, in search of our better selves."

The First History Man

For Kofo,

the only heart strong enough to truly beat, for two

i am sitting in the same place I know is safe,
how have I gotten here ?
where can I think to go ?
it's not even a lonely road anymore,
so I'll never get the rave
let me tell you what I've observed
well, what I've actually come to know…

these tears are not enough to wash away my guilt

my heavy heart cannot be unburdened by forgiveness

i am not strong enough to hold the torch that was handed to me

because my gratitude is not sufficient for my lack of involvement

i suppose that is a child's fantasy

but i must be selfish to become whole,

lest i lose myself forever

light of the world mine to harness
shining through panes, my ticket to glory

                  - a sunny summer through my window

"Love is the death of duty"
but if our affection leads us to an upper echelon
then let certain death give us our right to be free

                                        - thank you Maester Aemon

i have sat at the table of jesters
i have walked amongst the crowds of deceit
i have toiled in the fields of regret
i have lain in the bed of shame
i have bathed in the rivers of my tears
and laughed at the idea that no one cares
i have fallen on the sword of my own downfall
and ended my journey before it even began

- get out of your head :(

the rain falls angrily
stomping on the concrete, pounding the drums of war
spreading tales of hot disdain, and seeking retribution
the rain, does not act at my behest
but i am helpless to calm it,
imprisoned by the shackles of my pain.
the rain will not listen to my plea
my wants, and desires lost in its thunderous rage
so, i join it; dancing & crying.
the rain pounds the drums of war,
and i embolden it as i writhe to the beat
becoming one,
as both our pains transform,
and are now lost, to the rhythm of revenge!

i sit at the spot we met
the wind softly ruffles my hair
as it forcefully takes me back to the spring in March before ___ left
i painfully dwell on the memories of when we were a pair
i gasp, and with learned reflex, reach out
i've become a warrior with no skills
i can't hold on to the good days because,
i was barely alive, even at our getaway in the hills.
"it was my fault", i would say
only because i knew my "soulmate"
would never have me doubt our love, my love, the…love.
the wind howls, loudly this time, ruffling my whole body
my attention is brought to the tears that have fallen
both past, and present.
there is a pain in my body
but i cannot place it
and i cannot place it because i cannot remove it
i cannot remove it because it is a pain from a love
that was supposed to be eternal.
isn't that cosmic ? eternal ?
i will live with this pain for eternity
because i had to become a warrior
for a battle i could not fight, and a war i would not win.
i will transmute with my scars
because, i refuse to be the result of the inability to love
so i sit at the spot where we met
giving myself to the wind, letting these tears renew me,
as i finally allow myself to be free of my fears

i am always near you, but we're so far apart
i'm reaching out, hoping to catch a glimpse of your heart
i cross these oceans daily, with no end in sight
i climb your mountains, wishing i could take flight
i'm surrounded by the rays of your essence
tell me, why does it feel like loving you is wrong ?
i cease to breathe at the mere thought of you
save me my love, our moments are so few
because i'm always near you & fate has set us apart,
but darling, i will settle,
for your imprint on my heart

the book never read-the boy/girl who's never loved/been loved

don't look at me
don't wander my way
don't have any thoughts about me
don't even think of picking me up
leave the dust where it falls, it adorns me well
don't let the sun shine on me
don't let my name escape your lips
leave my memory where it is: forgotten
no one has ever seen me
no one ever will see me
my pages have never been turned
and my heart has never been loved.
don't look at me
because my dear, life is content
when you haven't been defiled
by the hands of many

- waiting for my prince/princess charming

i didn't ask for the cards i was dealt,
but i can't give them back.
i haven't been given the faintest of chances,
but i cannot for one second even complain
so i have to bottle it up
and wear my pretty smile.
look alive, life is good
but if i have to play at this table
then the only way i will play,
is to throw it in disarray.
let my madness pacify me
for the effects of the choices,
i never got to make

whoever said fighting for love was easy,
never had to seek peace from love

break into my very core
in there will you find the scared little boy
who just wants to be loved

Imagine a world where you meet the perfect person
bringing constant joy, and happiness with their presence
unbeknownst to me, the impact his friendship would have
killing all my doubts that i am not worthy of being loved
uniting souls that would have otherwise remained alone
never can my gratitude be enough for my thanks
      little did you both know that,
Sailing on the adventure that is our friendship,
allows me to be my true self even when i'm weakened by it.
daring myself to be the epitome of altruism.
imagine a world where you've met the perfect persons
quieting the universe while keeping me alive.

                                  thank you, best friends

so you want to haunt me in the light
no! this victory is not yours.
i will keep you in the dark because
my soul,
is not yours to have

- dear toxic ex

how do you whisper sweet nothings, and get me to undress my heart ?
how do you caress me, and pull out caged words ?
how do you pore into my eyes to casually stare at my soul
how is it that your absence leaves me in despair ?
how is it that i want you more without you inside me ?
how can one human hold so much power ?
but no,
no, i do not complain.
i'm merely amazed
that my heart can be in sync with yours,
loving me for all i am
and all i can never be

i've been a burden for so long
never asking, but always needing
and you wonder why
i enjoy my lonesome

i had already caused myself to fail
you just came along to make sure
it was a job well done

i've kept my mouth shut for so long
so much so that these secrets are my very essence.
what used to be my burden, has now become my pillar,
my new weightlessness, my new normal.
if i dared to spill any, then i would cease to exist
please,
let me be...

when i look into our past, i remember our pain
when i look into our future, all i see is more pain.
but right now with you, is bliss.
i'm lost in the fantasy of our perfectly failed love
and i'm helpless to leave.
dear me, save you

people compromise happiness a lot. why ?

the pursuit of happiness- within the confines of what is morally good, and right-

will sometimes be deemed selfish

but as they say, those who matter won't mind,

and those that mind certainly shouldn't matter

…often times we look to the world seeking magic, understanding, peace, and miracles

but my question is "why do we look for something that we already are ?"

i don't need your approval for validation of my life

you didn't create me, so you can't define me

i don't live by the parameters of your societal expectations

i am a being, a sentient, a truth

i am not less than, i am not more than

i simply am

i am enough

- excerpt from my 22nd birthday caption

i love it when you dream
but dreams are expensive
so don't do it at my expense
because i'm barely able to afford mine

my beating heart…weep no more
my aching bones…quiet your yammering
my staggering legs…fear is your ally
no one who ever ventured
lost everything
because knowing what it means to love, and be loved
will always be far better
than living in fairytales,
in hopes for something perfect
when we ourselves
embody imperfection

dear shame,

      i hope this meets you well. thank you for the many missed opportunities, and the endless nights of tears, because i simply wanted to feel alive. thank you for allowing me to wallow in self-hate.

      while i hated you for it, i don't anymore. i now embrace you. you will always be near and dear. and you will never take me back. i will use you to achieve my potential, and you will stay in your corner forever, knowing you are powerless, to affect me anymore.

yours sincerely,

your owner

silver jubilee

sometimes you change the way i feel,
and sometimes the way i feel is the darkest place
and sometimes the darkest place,
is the only place where we could discover something real

i feel unoriginal sometimes
what am i fashioned from ?
the only thing that comes to mind is 'brokenness'
maybe all my pieces were never together from the start
forced together from the ache of pain, and ego
now i wonder
how do i begin ?

i, who am benign to the horrors of this world,
constantly find myself a victim of its cruelty.
you, who stands by offering no condolences,
do not give me the hope of finality.
they, who are the perpetrators,
only deserve my hate, and should feel my pain.

i, who puts on a strong face, and a bold charisma,
am filled with overflowing tears, and hot disdain.
you, who starts to see beyond my facade,
let your sympathy flow through you to comfort me.
they, who are now tired of their taunt,
give me but a brief moment of escape to taste
what it's like to be free.

i, who now sees the dawn breaking a smile
at my strength, am given the necessary wings to fly.
and fly, fly away from the pain, and my mute silence, i shall.
you, and they are nothing under my feet as i soar ever higher.
and i, with the help of this cruel, cruel world,
have been allowed to taste a divine power.

and all the rest, though they try, will not escape this world's drama- its karma

- circle of karma
circa '13/ '14

Nirvana

do you see ?
can you feel it ?
it's right at your fingertips,
charging through every cell,
it's our home.
the place where no one can find us
where our love will be born,
and remain in its purest form,
forever
welcome home, to Nirvana

it's easy to die
it's even easier to live
what's really hard,
is being remembered,
when you have made no impact at all.
and that's the very worst thing
because your memory ends with you
like the hot summer air that encourages life,
but is all too quickly
forgotten

i'm still holding on to your pain
i'm still harboring your hate
i'm still the guardian of your dreams
i'm still the cleanser of your sins
i'm still the harbinger of all your good tidings
i'm still the quiet child who could never hurt you
i'm still the counselor that offers guidance on your journey
i'm still the shoulder for all your fallen tears
i'm still the echo of reassurance when you need clarity
still still still
still i do it out of nature, and not out of obligation nor duty,
but simply because i cannot escape myself
so please, when all your emotions gather to discuss me,
plead my case;
plead that i was there for each one of them
taking a backseat, just to make sure you're okay.
because if our bond is severed,
then my dear, that is our end, but my beginning.
because, I, will painfully move on

                                              - the life of a pisces

i sailed the wildest oceans bravely
i climbed the highest mountain undaunted by my doubts

i stumbled into the forest of the unknown, and emerged a champion
i've endured the blows of a brother,
and the scorn of a sister.
and every time each journey ended,
i couldn't help but ponder "was it all worth it ?"
at the outset of a new journey, i look up to the sky
wondering if she has the answers of tomorrow
the only comfort i have,
is to let the pain out through my tears

you say you sacrificed for my sake
but your sacrifice meant being enslaved to an ideal.
you say all you have are your fruits
but that shouldn't be all you have to show for living.
you say i don't tell you anything
but what confidence is there to allow me to be free ?
you look at me, and beam with pride
but all i see,
is defeat,
loneliness,
and a jaded prisoner

silver jubilee

how long will i live to watch you sleep ?

how long will i live to be mesmerized when you crease your brow ?

how long will i live for my heart to stop when i catch you staring ?

how long will i live to battle interlocking of fingers ?

how long will i live to witness your pure joy light up the room ?

how long will i live to feel you breathe life into me every time i hold you ?

how long will i live to feel my whole body awaken when you hold me ?

how long, is not enough.

it is unquantifiable.

instead, i'll ask myself

how do we continue our journey

when this life is inept to contain our love ?

i cannot look at you and see love anymore
that idea has been perverse to mean nothing.
battered hands, and shattered souls;
vile tongue, and ruling fear;
reasoned imprisonment, and pacified lies
that… is all you have taught me of love.
i cannot look at you and see love anymore
all i can give you,
are the remnants of what was once pure

i don't need you anymore
but you constantly pull me back.
i'm sorry if i've hurt you
but i must rip you from me
so i can reach the heavens.

why must i die to be born anew ?
why should pain be my gateway to happiness ?
and why does there have to be bad for there to be good ?
i don't understand
and i don't think i would want to understand
but i will rise from these ashes
and i will not be known as the phoenix.
i will be something transcendent,
i will be free

silver jubilee

a silent touch that crosses the wind
unknown to me, and unknown to you.
it will be all that we'll ever have,
the only memory of our fateful encounter

do you see the light ?
deep within the scars that will never heal.
have you lived in the darkness ?
locked away by the tears that forever run.
and have you finally realized
that you heart has never stopped to beat
and my dear do you know
that your pain has never truly existed ?
awaken !

how do you hold me with everything but your hands ?
how is it that the very sight of you,
leaves me with more words than i could ever speak
a tilt here, a chuckle there;
i'm forever mesmerized
she'll love you for who you're not
but i'll forever love you for who you're yet to acknowledge.
my E!

i stand in the shadow of our love
basking in the memories of our younger selves.
now i know that i had everything in needed,
but it was never enough for me.
i had a need to have more
i thought it all too good to be true
so i looked far and wide
searching in the smiles, and lies of strangers.
meandering my way through the loins of my conquests
while you were my pillar and shield
leaning only on you for learned support.
now i'm lying in the shame of my deceit
engulfed by the flames of carnal desires
left wanting with each passing encounter.
i now want more out of habit
but truth be told, the only thing i want is,
- you.
while i continuously search, i look for you in everybody
in my conquests, and in the lovers who have conquered me
i've found flashes of you in different people, but never the whole you
and while i had set out to look for you, i lost you in the process.
this will be my cross to bear, and i shall bear it forever
i'll continue to stand in the shadows of our ended love
where the sun will never shine, and out hearts will never beat as one

silver jubilee

rainfall, sunshine, haze, and snow

side by side, we've witnessed the changes in nature.

joy, sadness, laughter, and tears

together, we've braved the stormy weather of emotions.

growth, stagnancy, pain, and relief

the vows we took on that summer afternoon

have been put to the test.

and now, the boy i've known since we were babes

fades before my very eyes.

the memories we've made and shared are all that keep me strong

i do not know what life will be when you're gone.

but i do know that you breathed life into me

since our hearts became one all those years ago.

my darling, thank you for a life well lived.

i have been content to share a life with you,

and i take comfort in knowing that even if you won't be here,

your heart will always be joined with mine.

because husband, this love is till death does us both apart

- watching an older couple as they enjoy each others' embrace.

do not be gentle,
grab me.
do not be kind,
permeate every nook, and cranny.
do not let me run,
but chase me till i'm begging for mercy.
do not be slow,
awaken me with every thrust.
do not be bitter,
let me taste the sweetness of your every effort.
let us move together with rage guiding us,
as you shatter these plastered walls,
and infuse me with your energy.
it is not a race
but let us journey against each other.
i will not fight,
but shall bring you to submission.
because as we reach ever higher,
and your essence pours into me,
with the frustration of our inhibitions,
i will be a god.
and you will be but a mere mortal
fulfilling desires as old as time

silver jubilee

death does not scare me
having been unaccomplished…does

i look at you, and my heart swells
i think of you and my eyes weep
because my dear, i now have to dislike you

- welp

silver jubilee

you ask me to forget my pain,
but i've neglected everything else
this is all i am,
and it's all i have

i hope the sun darkens your path,

and i hope the moon brightens your darkness

i hope that when you reach your destination, you get lost in oblivion

and i hope that when you smile, your heart cries for freedom and peace

because life has more than eluded me, due to your selfishness

and this pain,

will not end its torment

- sincerely, the hurt

silver jubilee

do not waiver
do not falter
for if you slip for just a second
i will strike,
and i will be merciless

you put me down,
dragged me through the gutter
taunting me with my pain, but you forget.
this pain is a piece of me
it is a part of me i will carry forever
and it does not define me.
no matter how much you try,
your actions only speak of you,
and your insecurities

in the quest to look for everything
i found nothing but my own darkness.
i thought i had the light
but maybe,
just maybe
the dark is where i can be truly free

we've chosen happiness,
and accepted sadness
but deep down,
all we really want,
all anyone really wants,
is acceptance

here's where i tell you i've had enough
enough of your manipulation
enough of your screaming tears
enough of your misplaced anger
enough of your hatred
enough of your malady
enough of your happiness
and enough of you apathy.
here's where i tell you I've had enough
enough
of you

how many times do we have to ask "why ?"
how long is enough for these tears to continue ?
when does the sun actually rise from beyond the horizon ?
when will love be enough to be-still hate ?
it's much too heavy for any one heart
and even heavier for a collective of hearts
Mother Universe, let it all be worth it
we humbly ask

- our prayer across time

silver jubilee

Kindness from you is one that can never be repaid
out of every great deed done
few have been able to match the love
only your heart could fill to make mine whole.
when i thought i was hopeless, and unworthy of love
out of that desecrated darkness,
right at the core of my soul
our journey began to intertwine
leaving behind our pain
and ushering the age of peace, as we'd both once dreamed

let me hold your pain,
let me carry your burden
let me beguile your worries from you
though i only have one,
let my heart carry all that you want taken away

it's 5am and i cannot go back to sleep
i lie still, peering deep into the dark.
somehow, i hope for something to look back
but sadly, i am helpless to my own imagination.
i peer still, out of fascination
it's a wonder how,
oblivion can be so comforting

out of my own prison i emerge
trying to be brave, and strong
the first steps are always the hardest
even harder because my confinement was self-imposed
but there's been too much time wasted
too much of life has passed me by
so you see,
i simply cannot wait for tomorrow
let today, signify my rebirth

is it really that hard to look at me ?

have we grown so far apart that you mercy will always elude ?

do i even deserve the peace your heart offers ?

can i truly atone for my misgivings ?

i cannot open my mouth to utter these words.

i know what they are, and yet i'm simply,

too ashamed.

still, let these words offer you some comfort, my love

because even though i need to be at ease

i know you need it more.

darling,

forgive me…

we are the forgotten ones,
we are the overlooked angels.
we are the soul searchers
and the guardians of good.
we are the downtrodden and neglected
but the providers of safe haven.
we are the outliers,
we are the marooned.
we are the calm
holding in our storms.
we are the berated
and we are the welcomers.
we are the forgotten ones,
the ones who choose to believe.
because we are the ones
who know how to truly live.

                               - ode to glee. thank you, Mr. Schuester

every waking moment is bleak
the future i thought i once had no longer exists.
and this is through no fault of anyone,
not even destiny herself.
but life has lost control
so i desperately await each night
when i can crawl back into my dreams,
the safe harbor for lost realities
where life is bliss eternal,
my true world

let's get on our bikes, and ride down nevermore avenue
basking in the light of spontaneity
laughing in the face of adversity
and leaving behind the world that does not want us.
let's build a life on nevermore avenue,
our love, the unintended template,
offering hope and reassurance to those
who seek to find the everlasting
in their togetherness

beloved, you have come this far,
your heart deserves a break
put this book down for a second.
look to the distance,
keep looking,
breathe deeply,
hold that breath,
now slowly release,
with a smile.
now do you feel it ?
the aura of beauty and positivity that surrounds you.
beloved, you have come this far,
and all that goodness is made up of you,
and by you.
now breathe once more,
and smile again.

they say it gets better
but i haven't found my home since
i'm filled with strangers who are not present,
and i am helpless to banish them.
so, i'm forced to grow with them.
they share my every thoughts, and dance in my dreams
or is it my nightmares ?
truth be told,
i'd rather the devil i know
than the disguised angel,
with no respect for boundaries

                                                                                        - consent is real

silver jubilee

they had to crucify us, and send us to damnation
their feeble hearts could not handle our purity
but baby, on our way,
let our love scorch their precious earth
as we bow out
in the blaze of glory

shall i awaken when the pain subsides ?
or will my hurt cause the infection to wither away ?
i suppose i'll never know.
i'm not entirely sure if i'm awake or asleep.
this must be limbo

silver jubilee

let me tell you about me.
i was fashioned from the pains of my imperfections
broken by the failed promises of allies
shattered by the lack of identity,
and disposed by those who would wield their power brazenly

but let me really tell you about me
while i laid in tears, and rejection
cowering like a new born in oblivion,
i began to bloom
rebuilt by friendship,
emboldened by family,
and made whole with true love.

and no, i am not filled with light.
let me tell you about me.
i was born out of pure darkness,
restored by the goodness of others,
and rebirthed by my self will.
life, stood no chance against me,
and as such, the sweet taste of victory
could have only been mine to savor

bare your heart open
let me in that place no one has ever reached
pull me into you
pushing me away as i near dangerously.
satisfy your curiosity
and peak at both our arrival.
is this what ecstasy feels like ?

- fuck!

she carefully walks in the room
arms together, asking for comfort
as she in turn comforts herself.
every step is calculated
moving certain, as though for her sanity.
she tries to keep her head up
but it falls heavily, with grace.
there is an innocence in her
but its light shines dimly.
she paces across the room
desperately trying to fade away
but such beauty would not permit.
and as she crosses
she leaves her sorrows temporarily,
hoping that she can save herself
before anyone attempts to be the hero.
because while she may be a damsel filled with distress,
she damn sure is also her heroine

my favorite time is the middle of the night
the witching hours
where nothing happens
but life is abound
i can fade away,
feel totally alive,
and no one
will be the wiser

i'm sorry for holding your heart hostage
it's uncharacteristic of me.
but i just discovered myself,
so i'm not sure if it is my true nature.
i hate that i lost my best friend
but i know that
rebuilding your heart
cannot be done
by me

- your Achilles.

it took me less time to try and reach you.
panicked, brushing through the idleness,
and going as fast as i could.
hoping your heart was still connected to mine
so you could see,
that i exist only for you.
but as i got through the idleness,
i saw your back turned to me
letting me know all i needed.
time couldn't hold you much longer
as it pulled you quickly from the hurt
so your heart could begin to heal.
and i was left standing,
forced to face the demons,
of my own handiwork

    - it doesn't pay to eat your cake and have it too…

silver jubilee

the future scares me
not because you won't be in it,
but because i'm afraid i would leave you,
to go it alone

my growth shouldn't be your responsibility
but be patient with me
as you soar.
i'm only just getting my wings back
and i have to learn to fly again.

silver jubilee

how could i have been so lucky ?
to know the love of a mother
and that of a lover.
a person should have one heart,
but I've been blessed with 3
blessed
blessed
blessed

- listening to Stan x 6lack

"*stay*" i whisper softly out of habit
but my heart wants you to go.
we know we aren't good for each other,
but this toxicity is intoxicating.
and i'd rather die sick with your love
than be healthy
without you

i crossed that ocean
and climbed that fiery mountain.
i even braved the whispering forests
as the condescending fog descended upon me
but you weren't there…yet.
so i'll wait, as long as i need to
for us to be reunited again

solemnly i walk till the end of time
moving to the tune of your heartbeat
encapsulated by your gentle soul.
i daren't misstep
for if i do
our paths will jointly disintegrate
from trying to cling to one another
pulling further apart with each struggle
so let me hold on tightly,
i cannot bear the thought
of losing forever
to forever

i left it all behind, and never looked back
i rebuilt my scars to remind me where i came from
glistening them, so i never forget.
let me promise you,
no matter how hard you try,
you will never break me
because i was already broken,
and only i
was able to put my pieces
back together

                                                       - fuck off

so you were right
life hasn't been the same.
i lost the best thing,
but not only that
i lost me trying to be your everything.
and now, i can't find me anymore
i'm just an empty shell,
with the mission of a failed facade

i hate being indebted to people
yes, no man is an island.
but why should my progress
be tethered to another's assistance ?
free me,
cut me lose
set me free

i was walking down the path of uncertainty
when suddenly, i was asked, *"what is your greatest fear ?"*
and as i was about to answer, i halted.
not because i was caught unawares,
but because i didn't know what it was
i'm afraid of so many things
that nothing scares me more than the other
they just come, and go
as they please

here we go with your unsolicited opinion.
but i promise you,
you can keep it

i don't want to meet someone full of life.
beaming with the joy of a thousand happy suns.
give me an encounter with the soul that has no life,
who only exists because there is nowhere else to go.
because who would they lie to ?
who would they feign joy for ?
give me an encounter with the hopeless,
it is they, whose trust and friendship
can always be counted on

i guess the reason why my heart is so big,
and why i have so much to give,
is because i'm broken.
i have all these pieces that can never be whole again.
i might as well put them to good use
while they are still valuable

i'm not afraid of loving
i'm not even afraid of never being loved
i'm afraid,
that i'll never be afraid again

silver jubilee

you do not need anyone to complete you
you are a completion,
the completion.
your heart only needs its other match,
to bask in eternal togetherness

for the heart that's broken
for the heart that's rising again
that love just wasn't meant for you.
closing, and sealing that door meant,
and still means
that you have elevated your heart and self to that place,
that only you and your soulmate
could only ever reach

silver jubilee

all white like an angel
but my soul's black
yet, i'm not the devil.
my killer smile, a rehearsal
the light behind my facade, a mere tinsel.
i tried for years, and travelled for miles
to get you to find me within me
to find that white light, my light
but the darkness, oh the darkness and i,
are now whole.
a new species
that cannot exist
without the other

where are you going my love ?
what does your heart yearn for ?
where will your journey lead ?
if you have to leave,
take me with you
for living without you
is not life at all.
it is simply... existing

do you remember July
when all our fears and cares hated us ?
do you remember the hills
where the sun and moon bowed to our every wishes ?
do you remember the moment
where we knew what our mouths were too heavy to speak ?
and do you still dream of me
when you lay under the stars
reaching for what once was
but is no more ?

                                           - i miss you everyday

lie with me, if only for a moment
lie to me, even though truth scoffs at our denial
just spare me one more second
so that i could freeze us in time
before our pain and regret
fill what is left
of our damned hearts

HUMAN

what do i believe I am ?
i believe i'm strong.
but why is it, every time i want to do something,
i fall down?
the inability to feel among.
constantly gasping, and reaching;
snickers, and jests abound, leaving me helpless.
so i drown in a pool of pity and distraught,
but I still feel strong,
so where does it come from ?
it feels like a pull, a strong pull; oh, it's distant.
but i let it pull me, hoping to find some treasure, a kingdom,
where all is sweet, and free; joyful, and peaceful.
ow, i pinch myself; i'm already in a kingdom.
a kingdom that's exciting, intriguing;
igniting even though full of dreadfulness.
its inhabitants battling both angels, and demons
for how do I know bitterness without ever having known sweetness ?
and how do I feel free, without having been oppressed?
maybe there's an alternate world where there's a system
that goes according to how people want it.
but i won't fool myself;

i would die of boredom.
the singularity of nature, my fate;
a life of death, my end.
so, what do i believe i am ?
i believe I'm strong.
that feeling of weakness, of always falling down
is strength in itself.
it's almost comical, like watching a clown
for how do i know strength without weakness ?
i believe that it is nothing,
yet it makes me feel something… everything.
i believe that freedom is oppressed
and i also believe that every time I fall and drown,
that in some cosmic joke,
it's preparing me for the physical strength
that i mentally feel,
so i don't break down
when i actually get a taste of the strength first hand
i believe the word is 'Human';
i'm unbreakably boundless.

when i kiss you
it takes all in me not to shatter.
so i let out a whimper,
as i let your lies seep into me
erasing painful thoughts of infidelity
and planting seeds of doubt,
that'll bloom to convince me
that i am the crazy one

                              - why won't you let me go ?

i've convinced myself that you're still good.
so i hold on tightly to all our good memories,
while reality painfully claws at my soul
and i bury my pain
with sweet wishes of a tomorrow
that is never going to come

silver jubilee

i stood in front of the ocean today
and i cannot recall how long for.
all i remember thinking was,
will the water be enough,
to wash away all my fallen tears

i know someday, i will be free.
people ask why i stay
little do they know
it takes more courage to stay,
than it takes to leave.

or am i a prisoner ?

from zero to ten
life was pure bliss.
i maneuvered through life as though a newborn
unaware of the world that so carefully hid in the dark
waiting, like the fox that will descend on the henhouse.
i do cherish those moments
for if i haven't known them,
then i cannot have realized
what i have missed so dearly

who knew that from 11 and beyond the storm will never end ?

who could prepare me for the journey no one had ventured ?

that innocence could be so easily corrupted by maliciousness ?

i want to go back, but i'm forced to grow

forced to face the raging battle,

and my own consequences

who knew that 11 would mark the beginning of my need for a pen,

and the end of a world that knew no pain ?

i look at my heart, and he stares back

we've made it this far, and it has been long

but we have even further to go

we must soldier on

and now at the silver jubilee of my birth,
i find myself in the same place i know is safe
i know it's safe because even as i puzzled my next steps
i am not frightened.

with fear beside me as a friend, i look to the impending journey
the road ahead is not lonely, nor is it joyful
it's just a road;
a blank canvas.
all i've come to know points to one thing….
that i'm still unsure.
i'm sorry,
i thought i knew, but i don't.
the only thing i'm sure of,
is that i'm now 25

so here we are…the end

i thought putting these thoughts down would somehow heal me

but I'm still angry; lonely; confused; ashamed; and depressed

i look to the horizon for answers,

there are none in sight.

it isn't dire;

though i can't say i feel hopeful.

but here we are, my last words for my silver jubilee

i suppose i can call this,

the beginning.

- thank you x 25

i hope your journey here wasn't tumultuous. and i hope that you have some relief as the weight you could never put into words, elude you. thank you for your care of my heart. you mean more to me than you could imagine.

S.J

"nolite te bastardes carborundorum"
June/Offred

Illustrations by Rahmon Azeez

www.ingramcontent.com/pod-product-compliance
Lightning Source LLC
Chambersburg PA
CBHW011141290426
44108CB00023B/2715